12
INTIMIDATIONS

THE LIES SATAN USES TO HINDER OUR EVANGELISM

R. LARRY MOYER

This book is dedicated to those who want to know how Satan intimidates believers in evangelism and rebuke those intimidations by consistently sharing the good news.

Contents

THE 12 INTIMIDATIONS

Introduction

Intimidation. Satan is a master at it. In fact, nobody is better. He often does it through lies. So much so, that the Bible calls him a liar and the father of lies (John 8:44). And he tells those lies in such a way that you are convinced that he knows what he is talking about.

Nowhere does he enjoy intimidating people through lies more than in evangelism. Why wouldn't he? After all, when you share the good news of Christ with unbelievers, you are making a direct attack against his kingdom. If they should respond to your message and trust the Savior, his kingdom has suffered a decrease and God's kingdom has experienced an increase. It could be argued that nothing makes Satan angrier than to see a believer sharing the gospel. By virtue of the person trusting Christ, Satan has already lost one person, and now through that believer telling someone else about the Savior, he is about to lose another.

That is why he tries to get at us before we even begin by playing with our minds. He may have us reflect upon bad experiences or look at our failures in one area or another. If he can play with our minds, he feels he is at least "inside the door" in discouraging our evangelism.

However, Satan can do nothing in our lives unless God allows it. When He does, it is to make us more mature and Christlike. God is in control, not Satan. Any intimidation Satan tries has to be allowed by God for a good purpose.

These intimidation devices become excuses for not evangelizing and they are his primary tools. He has been using the same ones worldwide for years. He is actually not very original! There are twelve common intimidation devices he uses repeatedly. Sometimes they contain a bit of truth, but he misrepresents that truth to try to discourage and defeat us.

This book will inform you about the intimidation excuses Satan uses as well as how he uses them. With that understood, you can confront him directly, admonish him to move aside, and go on to have what could be the most enjoyable experience of your life— leading someone to the Savior. Even if the person you share the gospel with does not trust Christ, you will still have the thrill of knowing that you did not allow Satan to keep you from being God's representative in telling unbelievers something God wants them to hear loudly and clearly—I LOVE YOU!

Intimidation #1

You do not know the Bible well enough to evangelize.

Satan knows that you want to share the truth of God's Word with non-Christians. He also knows that you want everyone to understand that what you are saying comes from a higher source—God Himself. You are not presenting your plan of salvation; you are presenting His.

The intimidation he uses is, "You do not know the Bible well enough to evangelize." One thing Satan tries to cause us *not* to see is that people who know the Bible from cover to cover are not necessarily the ones that lead the most people to Christ. Instead, it is a brand-new convert—someone recently led to the Savior—because he wants everyone to know the truth that just changed his life. New converts are some of God's most zealous evangelists. I've known many who, within days of their conversion, got as many people together as they could to tell them the exciting message that just changed their lives.

Nowhere does the Bible say that you have to know the entirety of Scripture to evangelize. Rather, it is a *specific message* in the Bible that you need to understand. The message is the gospel and is called the "power of God unto salvation." Romans 1:16 tells us, "For I am not ashamed of the gospel of Christ, for it is the power of God to salvation for everyone that believes, for the Jew first and also for the Greek."

> New converts are some of God's most zealous evangelists.

The historical components of that message are defined in 1 Corinthians 15:3–5, where we read, "For I delivered to you first of all that which I also received: that Christ died for our sins according to the Scriptures, and that He was buried, and that He rose again the third day according to the Scriptures, and that He was seen by Cephas, then by the twelve."

Note the four verbs surrounding Christ: died, buried, rose, seen. His burial is proof that He died. One does not bury people who are alive but people who have died. The fact that He was seen is proof that He rose. Others saw Him following His resurrection. So, the basic truth of the gospel could be reduced to ten words: *Christ died for our sins and rose from the dead*.

It is *that* message unbelievers need to hear, not the entire Bible. If someone knows those ten words, *Christ died for our sins and rose from the dead*, they are prepared to talk to anyone anywhere. Once non-Christians hear that message, God is asking them to believe. He is asking them to respond in faith by trusting Christ alone as their only way to heaven. God's promise to those who trust Christ is, "Most assuredly, I say to you, he who believes in Me has everlasting life" (John 6:47).

> If someone knows those ten words, *Christ died for our sins and rose from the dead*, they are prepared to talk to anyone anywhere.

Knowing as much of the Bible as possible is always helpful in evangelism. If they ask you about a particular verse, you might be able to explain it. You also might be able to answer a particular question they have that the Bible addresses. But even if you taught them the entire Bible, and they received what you taught, this does not necessarily mean that they have come to Christ. It is when they receive the gospel, the truth about Christ's death and resurrection, *and trust Christ*, that they will be saved. Besides, as I will mention when we address another excuse Satan uses, if they ask you a question about something in the Bible that you have not yet learned, you can always say, "I do not know" and come back to them later with the answer.

While *knowing the entire Bible* isn't essential to evangelism, *knowing the Gospel* is. Relax in the fact that when you know the simple message that Christ died for our sins and rose from the dead, you are prepared to speak to those who need to hear that simple and life-changing message.

Questions for Reflection

1. When have you put too much pressure upon yourself to know more of the Bible before you shared your faith? Can you think of a specific time?

2. Why and how should the realization that if you know the ten words that constitute the gospel provide both relief and boldness in evangelism?

Intimidation #2

You will make a fool of yourself. You won't be able to answer their questions and objections.

This intimidation shows you how tricky Satan is. It is a lie that contains a half-truth.

Chances are that you will not be able to answer every question and objection. There are two reasons. First, how can you adequately prepare if you do not know what they are going to ask? You are not a mind reader. Secondly, if you are a new Christian, you may not have learned enough to be able to answer the questions and objections that some have. In fact, even those who have been believers for many years may not know how to answer particular questions or objections.

Nowhere in the Bible does it ever say that you have to know all of the answers. Most people do not have an encyclopedic knowledge of how to answer every question or objection that a non-Christian might have and yet many still lead others to the Savior. They are zealous about declaring Him. It is their zeal, not their intellect, which causes unbelievers to listen to them.

We are told in Acts 5:42 about the apostles, "And daily in the temple, and in every house, they did not cease teaching and preaching Jesus as the Christ." They wanted everyone to hear the good news of Christ's death and resurrection. Nowhere is a word said about their ability to answer questions and objections that could be raised. They just wanted to share the gospel with everyone. That is particularly interesting after they had been beaten for speaking in the name of Jesus (Acts 5:40).

> Nowhere in the Bible does it ever say that you have to know all of the answers.

Dawson Trotman who founded an association called the Navigators was noted for his statement, "Soul winners are not soul winners because of what they know but who they know and how much they want others to know Him."

However, Acts 17:2 says, "Then Paul, as his custom was, went in to them, and for three Sabbaths reasoned with them from the Scriptures." Paul knew how to answer questions and objections. This ability to answer questions and objections that many people have can be a great help in evangelism. But nowhere does the bible call that a requirement for evangelism.

What Satan also does not tell you is that there are three words that are winsome with unbelievers if they raise a question or an objection that you are not able to answer. Those three words are, "I don't know." You might also say, "Let me think about that." Comments like those demonstrate both honesty and humility—qualities that a non-Christian can respect. You can then look up the answer and be prepared for the next time you have a chance to interact with the person and the next time that question arises. That way anyone may catch you once without the answer to a particular question, but nobody will catch you twice.

The more you share your faith and hear any questions and objections unbelievers raise and learn the answers, the better equipped you become in evangelism. The particular question you were not able to answer the first time, you will be able to answer the next time.

Of course, Satan does not want you to know that many people will not have any particular questions or objections. They have simply not had someone explain the gospel clearly to them. If you ask them, "Has anyone ever taken a Bible and shown you how you can know you are going to heaven," they will likely respond,

"No, I don't believe they have." Furthermore, God's love is expressed clearly by His substitutionary death (They crucified Him when they should have crucified us) and His resurrection. The fact that He would actually take their place on a cross as their substitute often makes their questions and objections less important to them.

> The more you share your faith and hear any questions and objections unbelievers raise and learn the answers, the better equipped you become in evangelism.

Satan loves to twist Scripture out of context to reinforce his excuses. One Scripture he loves to use is 1 Peter 3:15. We read, "But sanctify the Lord God in your hearts, and always be ready to give a defense to everyone who asks you a reason for the hope that is in you, with meekness and fear." So, in essence, Satan says, "See, even the God you are talking about says that you should not talk to others about Him unless you can answer any questions or objections they raise."

That is *not* what that passage is saying. In looking at the context, Peter is arguing that we should always suffer for doing right not wrong. He said a few verses earlier, "And who is he who will harm you if you become followers of what is good?" *Usually*, it is evildoers that face harm for their actions, not good doers. At the same time, he continues, "But even if you should suffer for righteousness' sake, you are blessed. And do not be afraid of their threats, nor be troubled." In other words, do not let them intimidate you.

Why and how? His answer is to let a proper fear of God drive out our fear of man—"sanctify the Lord God in your hearts." Then when people ask you, "Why are you not afraid?" or "Why do you even believe in God?" or "Why do you serve one God instead of many?" you can give "a reason for the hope that is in you, with meekness and fear." "Meekness and fear" mean reverence for God and respect for men. But in no way is that passage saying that we must be able to defend what we believe before we evangelize.

> Concentrate on *declaring* what you believe not on being able to *defend* what you believe.

Let me make a suggestion. Recognize that excuse for what it is—an instrument Satan wants to use to keep you from talking to anyone anywhere. Go ahead and share your faith. If a question comes up that you are unsure how to answer, just say, "May I write that down? Then when I am through explaining what I am so concerned that you understand, we will go back to it." That will prevent you from getting distracted. It is amazing how many times when you later offer to go back to their question, they say, "Oh, it is really not that important." Or if it is one you sincerely do not know how to answer, you can respond, "Let me write that down. I do not know the answer to that question, but I will do some study and get back to you."

Concentrate on *declaring* what you believe, not on being able to *defend* what you believe. The more you share your faith, you will increasingly develop a know-how in answering questions and objections. But it is Who you know, not how much you know, that will enable you to impact unbelievers.

Questions for Reflection

1. When have you been in a situation where upon being asked a question you could not answer, saying "I don't know" is all you would have needed to say?

2. How many times have you actually been asked a question you could not answer?

Intimidation #3

You are too much of a hypocrite. You don't even live the life you should.

Satan knows that if he can get you to believe this one, you will never talk to anyone about Jesus.

The reason is simple. Who on any given day would say that our lives have been 100% what they ought to be for Christ? There is no perfect Christian; there is only a perfect Christ. At the end of any day, we can look back and see such things as: we could have been more patient, our prayer life left a lot to be desired, we hurried through our Bible study, we were too often selfish and self-centered, our mind entertained the wrong thoughts, our tongue was not under control, and we passed up many opportunities to be kind to hurting people.

So, if you wait until your life is everything it ought to be, you will probably never say a word to anyone about the Savior. In fact, the more conscientious you are about your walk as a Christian, the more your failures could actually hold you back from evangelizing.

Furthermore, there is one huge thing Satan is not telling you that anyone who has spent as much time in evangelism as I have learns quickly. That is, unbelievers are not turned off by people who fail. They do not expect you to be perfect. They expect you to be honest. So, if they cite an area where you do not live as you should, simply say, "That is an area of my life I am not proud of and need to ask the Lord to make me a better person. I am very sorry if that has offended you or hurt my testimony with you." You will be amazed at how meaningful that is to them.

That is not to say you should not seek to change those things that would hurt your testimony. We ought to take seriously the admonition found in Philippians 2:14–15. "Do all things without complaining and disputing, that you may become blameless and harmless, children of God without fault in the midst of a crooked and perverse generation, among whom you shine as lights in the world." The impact your life has when you live the way you should cannot be overstated.

I once had the privilege of leading a car salesman to Christ who was impacted by a person whose name was also Larry. The car dealer said to me, "Most

Christians I knew did not live any better than I did. But Larry was the first one I met who really lived the life he preached." Larry's life was used of the Lord to begin making the car salesman think seriously about Christ.

> So, if you wait until your life is everything it ought to be, you will probably never say a word to anyone about the Savior.

Additionally, if Satan tries to use this accusation, it does not take a year to change the way you live. Admit that there may be truth about the hypocrisy of your life. Ask God to help you change that *today* so your life becomes an attraction not a deterrent to those who do not know the Lord. Strive to be what James 1:22 calls a "doer of the Word."

Involved in this intimidation is another element Satan is not telling you. Non-Christians are fully aware that their own lives have a lot of hypocrisy about them. A person to whom I witnessed told me that he would not become a Christian because if he did, he thought he should probably go to church. He then explained that he thought there were too many hyp-ocrites there. He was an avid baseball fan and was watching a game as we spoke. I gave him the name of a player whom I personally knew claimed to be a Christian (whom he liked) but was known in his home area as a hypocrite. I asked if he would allow me to turn off the TV because of players who are hypocrites. He refused. I asked him, "Then why do you not go to church because you cannot stand Christians who are hypocrites, but you do not mind watching this player play baseball, although he is a hypocrite? So, who is the bigger hypocrite—you or him?" Interestingly enough, he did not have an answer. Unbelievers who have been blinded by Satan (2 Cor. 4:4) often do not realize how they contradict themselves and give excuses rather than explanations for not coming to Christ.

> Non-Christians are fully aware that their own lives have a lot of hypocrisy about them.

When Satan uses this accusation, there is a further item he hopes does not come to your mind. God is not asking anyone to trust Christians. The most perfect Christian will not take you to heaven. God is asking you to trust Christ. He was not a hypocrite. Hypocrites don't die for you on a cross. Romans 5:8 tells us, "But God demonstrates His own love toward us, in that while we were still sinners, Christ died for us."

Even His enemies found no fault in Him. We are told in Luke 23:13–14, "Then Pilate, when he had called together the chief priests, the rulers, and the people, said to them, 'You have brought this Man to me, as one who misleads the people. And indeed, having examined Him in your presence, I have found no fault in this Man concerning those things of which you accuse Him.'"

> The most perfect Christian will not take you to heaven. God is asking you to trust Christ.

Live a life that attracts people to the Savior. But do not let Satan's accusations keep you from sharing the One who had no hypocrisy about Him.

Questions for Reflection

1. How does admitting your faults but not being held back by them, help you overcome this intimidation Satan uses?

2. How ought the realization that you are presenting a perfect Christ (not a perfect Christian) increase your boldness in evangelism?

Intimidation #4

They are going to be offended, and you will lose a good friend.

Notice how many of the excuses that Satan tried to get us to use are couched in language that implies, "This is *certain* to happen." With this excuse, he usually does not say you might lose a friend, but instead, you *will* lose a friend.

First of all, suppose you do. Genuine love puts the other person first even if it means the sacrifice of yourself. From an eternal perspective, what matters the most? Whether they have a relationship with *you* or with *Christ*? Obviously, first and foremost is their relationship with Christ. Their relationship with you will not obtain them eternal life. A relationship with Christ will result in being in His presence forever. John 1:12 tells us, "But as many as received Him, to them He gave the right to become children of God, to those who believe in His name." You do not want to lose a friend, but if that should happen and later they come to Christ, as they recall the truth you shared, it will be worth it all.

> From an eternal perspective, what matters the most? Whether they have a relationship with you or with Christ?

Relationships and friendships are built on care and concern. That is why you will most likely not lose a friend if he or she is approached in the right way. Sure, your friend does not want you to cram Jesus down her throat. But people who care for one another do not approach each other that way. Instead, their approach is, "Years ago, I was introduced to someone who changed my life and because of what happened, I now have no question where I am going when I die. I want you to have that same assurance so I would love to explain to you what someone explained to me." Knowing you care for them could make all the difference as you bring up spiritual matters.

Something Satan never addresses when he leverages that excuse (because it is something that terrifies him to no end) is the subject of prayer. Satan is not about to tell you that God is more concerned about your friend than you are. That is why when you bathe your friend in prayer, asking God for an opportunity to share, exciting things often happen. God causes events to come into their lives or thoughts to come into their minds that prepare them for your conversation. It is said that "Satan trembles when he sees the weakest Christian on his knees." Nowhere is that more true than when you talk to God before even talking to your friend.

Satan well knows the truth of 1 John 4:4, ". . . He who is in you is greater than he who is in the world." Many believers have seen a friend most approachable because of the way God, in response to prayer, prepared their heart and mind for the conversation. Ask God to provide that "door of opportunity" and you may be surprised by what happens.

Satan also does not want you to comprehend the power of grace and truth. John 1:14 tells us, "And the Word became flesh and dwelt among us, and we beheld His glory, the glory as of the only begotten of the Father, full of grace and truth." Suppose as you approach the subject, they appear to be offended. Truth and grace say, "Please know that I do not want to offend you. You are too good a friend for that. But it bothers me that caring for you as I do, I have not asked you about your interest in spiritual things. I promise you, though, it will not change our friendship either way." That combination of grace and truth is powerful in evangelism.

Satan also does not want you to understand the "norm" or, in other words, what is more likely to happen. The more normal experience is unbelievers will ask, "Why did you not talk to me about this sooner?" There again is a place for grace and truth. It is an opportunity for you to say, "I sincerely wanted to but not being certain of your interest or response, I was hesitant. Your friendship means a lot to me."

> Ask God to provide that "door of opportunity" and you may be surprised what happens.

See Satan's tactic for what it is—a fear of what probably won't even happen. Take the "*will* lose a friend" and change it to "*might* lose a friend." That means there is the possibility, not the probability, that it will happen. You might find yourself wishing you had approached the friend sooner. But if the conversation becomes uncomfortable, God through His Holy Spirit will help you know how to handle it.

Think about it. Satan wants you to capitalize on the possibility of losing a friend. What Satan is not telling you is that you "might gain a brother or sister in Christ."

Questions for Reflection

1. How and where have you concentrated too much on their relationship with you instead of their relationship with Christ?

2. How should the difference between thinking, "I might lose a friend" and "I will lose a friend" impact your evangelism?

Intimidation #5

You ought to wait until they bring up the subject so that you can tell if they are interested in spiritual things.

I am convinced that one of Satan's favorite words is "wait."

When it comes to sharing the gospel, he loves to say, "Don't do today what you can put off until tomorrow." Obviously, he knows that "tomorrow" may never come. With this excuse he can cause you to put off sharing the gospel until it is eternally too late because of their death or yours.

We believers, take our orders from Jesus, not from Satan. Where in the Bible does it say that you have to wait until they bring up the subject before you can approach an unbeliever about spiritual things? In the familiar story of Christ and the Samaritan woman of John 4, Christ initiated the conversation. She expressed surprise that He, as a Jew, would ask for a drink from her, as a Samaritan. He immediately said, "If you knew the gift of God, and who it is who says to you, 'Give Me a drink,' you would have asked Him, and He would have given you living water" (v.10).

Also, there are many times unbelievers have been hopeful that a Christian would approach them first. A doctor in the Northwest told me that after treating a patient, he told her that he was finished but she just sat there. Curious if there was anything else on her mind, he asked, "Is there something else?" She answered, "You mean that you are not going to talk to me about Jesus? One reason I made this appointment is that I heard you are a Christian. I have some questions about God and was hopeful you would bring up the subject." Unbelievers are not always sure how to approach the subject. Sometimes they hope you will bring it up first.

We, as believers, take our orders from Jesus, not from Satan.

While it may be true that a person may indeed *not* be interested in spiritual things, you could be the first one God uses to cause her to begin thinking about Him. When asked, "Have you thought much about spiritual things?" many unbelievers say, "No, I really haven't, but I probably need to." That first conversation is what ultimately leads some of them to the Savior. God uses some people as the last person in the line of those who are going to lead a person to the Savior. But sometimes, you could be the very first in a whole line of believers God is going to use.

> When Satan says, "Wait", we ought to respond by saying, "Watch!"

Satan is hopeful that many believers never come upon the truth expressed in Ecclesiastes 3:11, where we are told that God has given everyone a hunger to know what happens in the afterlife. We read, "He has made everything beautiful in its time. Also He has put eternity in their hearts, except that no one can find out the work that God does from beginning to end." So, everyone has thought about that at one time or another. Knowing that truth should encourage us to bring up the subject, not wait for them to do so.

When Satan says, "Wait," we ought to respond by saying, "Watch!" In obedience to your assignment as a disciple to be a "fisher of men" (Matthew 4:19), ignore Satan's lie and speak to them about their need of Christ.

Questions for Reflection

1. How might the idea of "tomorrow" instead of "today" cause you to neglect opportunities to evangelize this week?

2. Can you think of anyone you have met that when they were a non-Christian wanted to discuss spiritual things but did not know how to bring up the subject?

Intimidation #6

You are not very good at explaining things. You may do more harm than good.

Satan knows your weak spots. So, one of his lies is to attempt to show you how that weak spot will apply to evangelism.

You may indeed not be good at explaining things. Many people are not. I love (and laugh at) the story of the woman who went to a judge seeking a divorce. The judge asked her, "On what grounds do you want a divorce?" The woman answered, "My husband and I have about an acre and a half. I would like it to cover the whole thing." The judge responded, "You do not understand. What I mean is, do you have a grudge?" She answered, "Yes, we have a two-car one. He keeps his on the left, and I keep mine on the right." The judge said, "Ma'am, you still do not understand. What I am trying to find out is, has he ever beat you up?" She answered, "He has never beat me up. I am up before him every single morning." The judge said, "You still do not understand. What I am trying to find out is, why do you want a divorce?" She answered, "I don't understand it either, but he says I can't communicate."

Some people are just not good at explaining things! Communication is not where they are at their best. Satan's lie goes—so, since you are not good at explaining things, you won't be good at explaining this either.

One word Satan tries to dismiss from your mind is "training." Many do not feel confident in how to explain the three things one needs to know to come to Christ. They are: (1) we are sinners; (2) Christ died for us and rose again; and (3) we have to trust in Christ alone to save us. Evangelism training has helped many know how to explain those three truths to an unbeliever. Additionally, there are attractive tracts in paper and online that one simply has to read through with an unbeliever. The tracts themselves do the explaining.

Evangelism training has also helped believers know how to transition a conversation into spiritual things and even answer some particular questions an unbeliever might have. Those are areas Satan often uses to intimidate Christians in evangelism.

The biggest thing Satan does not want you to see is that, when you engage in sharing your faith, you are not doing it alone. Six of the greatest words (found in what is commonly referred to as the Great Commission in Matthew 28:20) are, "Lo, I am with you always." God is more concerned about the explanation of His good news to the lost than you are. A simple prayer of "God, help me explain this clearly" is all it takes to experience His divine help.

But Satan is not one who goes halfway—he loves to add a lie to a lie. He continues by saying, "You may do more harm than good." *That has never happened.* There are two reasons. God is bigger than your mistakes and those mistakes do not prevent Him from bringing someone to Christ. Secondly, God uses your mistakes to teach you. Those who share Christ often do it the best because they learn as they share.

> The biggest things Satan does not want you see is that, when you engage in sharing your faith, you are not doing it alone.

Furthermore, suppose you do what Satan calls "harm." Perhaps you rush into a conversation too quickly or aburptly respond to a non-Christian's comment. Once more, God is bigger than your mistakes. He can overcome them to bring the person to Christ. Most importantly, God is not asking you to bring the lost to Christ but instead to bring Christ to the lost. The non-Christian can use something you said or did as an excuse for not coming to Christ, but that is all that is—an excuse. Should that person not come to Christ, God does not hold you responsible for their eternal separation from God. That is never stated in the Bible.

Sometimes Satan uses Scripture taken out of context to make us think that we are responsible for someone's eternal destiny. One of those Scriptures often misused is Ezekiel 3:18–19. We read, "When I say to the wicked, 'You will surely die,' and you give him no warning, nor speak to warn the wicked from his wicked way, to save his life, that same wicked man shall die in his iniquity; but his blood I will require at your hand. Yet, if you warn the wicked, and he does not turn from his wickedness, nor from his wicked way, he shall die in his iniquity, but you have delivered your soul."

A simple prayer of "God, help me explain this clearly" is all it takes to experience His divine help.

That verse has nothing to do with evangelism. The death spoken of is physical, not spiritual. The context is the Babylonian destruction of Jerusalem that Ezekiel predicted. Ezekiel had been appointed a watchman over Israel to warn them of impending danger. Chapters 4–24 contain his cry of alarm. Had he not warned them, he would be responsible for their deaths. But by warning them, even if they ignored his warning, they were responsible for their own deaths and Ezekiel saved himself from the responsibility of the coming judgment. Once more, the verse has nothing to do with evangelism.

> The non-Christian can use something you said or did as an excuse for not coming to Christ but that is all that is—an excuse.

Let God use you to explain His good news to others. Recognize that regardless of what happens, you have ultimately honored the Lord and helped both yourself and others. You have gained experience by explaining something they need to know. Even if it could have been said or done better!

Questions for Reflection

1. How and where can you grasp training opportunities this month that will help you to better communicate your faith to others?

2. How has the fear of making a mistake been prevalent in your mind when faced with witnessing opportunities?

Intimidation# 7

At times you question your own salvation. You cannot talk about their salvation when you are unsure of your own.

Satan loves to mix an ounce of truth with a ton of lies.

You *can* talk to others about their salvation if you are not sure of your own, but you are unlikely to do so. Therein lies an ounce of truth. How can you enthusiastically share with others how to get to heaven when you are not certain you will be there yourself? Besides, it is hard to focus on their struggle if you are preoccupied with your own.

Where the "ton of lies" comes in is that Satan gives you the impression that the assurance of their salvation is dependent upon the assurance of yours. In other words, you believe the lie that they cannot be certain of their salvation until you are certain of yours.

If they receive your message of grace and trust Christ, they are as certain of heaven as if they are already there. Even if you struggle with assurance of your salvation, there is no need for them to struggle with theirs. Those are two separate matters because you are talking about two different people. Satan loves to confuse issues!

Where the "ton of lies" also comes in is that Satan gives you the impression that since you may always lack assurance, you should give up permanently on the thought of evangelizing. Put yourself in Satan's shoes. If you can torment someone with a lack of assurance of salvation, would you ever want to *stop* tormenting them? Of course not. A temporary roadblock to sharing their faith becomes a permanent one.

Satan loves to confuse issues!

What God wants you to do is say, "Get behind me, Satan," and ask the question, "Why am I unsure?" It could be for any number of reasons. Perhaps you cannot remember the actual date you came to Christ and someone told you, "If you do not know the date you were saved, then you are not saved." Biblically, that is not true. If you are trusting Christ alone to save you, you are His forever regardless of when and where it happened.

Perhaps you have been told, "If you don't look and act like a Christian, then you are not a Christian." Again, nowhere in Scripture is that taught. Every believer has days when they do not look and act as they should as a Christian. But our assurance of salvation is based on His performance on a cross when He died for us, not on our performance.

You may have thought, "But sometimes I do not feel saved." Salvation is based on fact, not feeling. Some days you feel saved more than other days, but assurance of eternal life is based on a promise from a God who cannot lie. It has nothing to do with your feelings. John 5:24 tells us, "Most assuredly, I say to you, he who hears My Word and believes in Him who sent Me has everlasting life, and shall not come into judgment, but has passed from death into life." He promised that when you trust Christ, that settles it—forever.

Ask yourself these three questions. Do I admit I am a sinner who deserves eternal separation from God in what the Bible calls hell? Do I understand that Jesus Christ as the perfect Son of God took my place on a cross suffering the punishment for my sins on the cross and rose again? Am I trusting Christ alone as my one and only way to heaven?

If the answer to those is "yes" then take God at His Word. 1 John 5:13 tells us, "These things have I written to you who believe in the name of the Son of God, that you may know that you have eternal life. . ." If Satan has an argument with your salvation, he is talking to the wrong person. Satan's argument is with God, not with you. Again, He said it and that settles it.

> Satan's argument is with God, not with you.

With that assurance, go talk to anyone and everyone about their salvation. Any time the thought, "Am I saved myself?" comes to your mind, go back to God and His promise—nothing else. Any struggle you have had about your salvation will soon be behind you. Satan will learn that if he is going to use that intimidation to keep a believer from sharing his faith with others, it will have to be someone other than you.

Questions for Reflection

1. Why should the matter of an unbeliever's salvation and yours be two separate issues?

2. How might you have allowed Satan to argue with you about your salvation instead of directing him to God?

Intimidation #8

This may not be a good time. You probably do not know half of what is happening in their lives.

Sometimes Satan is a master of the understatement. The truth is that you do not know *most* of what is happening in their lives, not merely one half! For practically everyone that we have an opportunity to speak to, we do not know most of the circumstances surrounding their lives.

The truth is that you really do not need to know *anything* about their lives. Many people share the gospel with complete strangers. In fact, not knowing much about their lives can sometimes be an advantage. It allows you to ask questions about their family, job, and background. As you do so, you discern ways that you can move the conversation from the secular to the spiritual and ultimately to the gospel.

Satan also does not want you to know that God knows everything that is happening in their lives. There is nothing He does not know. In John 2:24–25, we are told, "But Jesus did not commit Himself to them, because He knew all men, and had no need that anyone should testify of man, for He knew what was in man." God, in wanting to draw a person to Christ, may have brought you along just at this time because He is preparing them for your conversation. He, in His divine love and providence, knows "Now is the time."

The disciples were surprised when they came to Samaria and found people ripe and ready for the gospel, probably because of the ministry of John the Baptist or the Old Testament prophets. Hence, Christ encouraged them, "Do you not say, 'There are still four months and then comes the harvest?' Behold, I say to you, lift up your eyes and look at the fields, for they are already white for harvest" (John 4:35).

A good question to ask Satan is, "When is a good time?" That will show you what a devil he is because his answer is "never." It is bigger than the fact that now may not be a good time. As far as Satan is concerned, there will *never* be a good time. He does not want you talking to someone about the Savior now or ever.

As addressed earlier, two of Satan's favorite words are "wait" and "tomorrow." He knows that if he can get you to succumb to that kind of thinking, tomorrow will never come. What you put off from doing today you are likely to put off forever.

> A good question to ask Satan is,
> "When is a good time?"

Before we came to Christ, Satan so blinded our eyes to the gospel that, unless the Holy Spirit had worked, we would have never seen our need of Christ. 2 Corinthians 4:3–4 tells us, "But even if our gospel is veiled, it is veiled to those who are perishing, whose minds the god of this age has blinded, who do not believe, lest the light of the gospel of the glory of Christ, who is the image of God, should shine on them." That blindness is removed when we come to Christ so that we can now understand spiritual truth. Hence, we are told, "But the natural man does not receive the things of the Spirit of God, for they are foolishness to him; nor can he know them, because they are spiritually discerned" (1 Corinthians 2:14). Although we are no longer blinded, Satan does his best through this intimidation to cause us not to recognize two things.

One is that the person we are talking to is not promised tomorrow. That fact is why there must be an urgency about our witness. I know of many who came to Christ a day, week, month, or year before they died unexpectedly. But the second is that *we* are not promised tomorrow. A man who went through our evangelism training led a friend to Christ one day before he himself died. Had he waited any longer, he would have missed that opportunity.

God warns us of how quickly life can end in James 4:13–15, "Come now, you who say, 'Today or tomorrow we will go to such and such a city, spend a year there, buy and sell, and make a profit;' whereas you do not know what will happen tomorrow. For what is your life? It is even a vapor that appears for a little time and then vanishes away. Instead, you ought to say, 'If the Lord wills, we will live and do this or that.'" Therefore, if God provides an opportunity to share the gospel, we should not procrastinate.

But there is a final thing Satan does not tell you. He may be right. *Now actually may not be a good time.* But how do you know unless you approach the subject? In grace, if you discern that now is not the best time, you can always back off and seek another opportunity.

Therefore, if God provides an opportunity to share the gospel, we should not procrastinate.

Let Christ and the particular circumstances tell you whether or not now is the best time. It may or may not be. But that timing and decision need to be the result of your walk with the Lord, not an intimidation tactic on Satan's part.

Questions for Reflection

1. You and the person you are talking to are not promised tomorrow. How should this impact every witnessing opportunity you have?

2. How should the idea that you can always back off, when necessary, encourage your boldness to go forward in evangelism?

Intimidation #9

You are trying to do something God uses gifted evangelists or those with better speaking skills to do. You don't have Bible college or seminary training.

Satan loves traditional thinking, especially when it allows him to intimidate or deceive.

A traditional thought in many people's minds is that sharing the gospel is something God wants pastors and evangelists to do, or at a bare minimum those with speaking skills. What others need to do is simply invite them to church where a pastor or evangelist can present the gospel through his sermon. After all, isn't that why a person in ministry goes to Bible college or seminary—to learn how to evangelize?

What Satan doesn't want you to know is what many in the body of Christ have learned. What the body of

Christ has come to recognize is that anyone who serves the Lord (wherever he may be) is in full-time ministry. Some are paid as Christian workers to free them up to serve in various ministries full or part-time. But anyone who serves the Lord (wherever they are and whatever they are doing) is in full-time ministry.

Satan would rather you not be introduced to Bezalel in the Old Testament. It is said of him in Exodus 31:1–3, "Then the Lord spoke to Moses, saying, 'See, I have called by my name Bezalel the son of Uri, the son of Hur, of the tribe of Judah. And I have filled him with the Spirit of God, in wisdom, in understanding, in knowledge, and in all manner of workmanship.'" Bezalel was a workplace leader, not a preacher, and yet he was filled with the Spirit of God. He was in full-time ministry in the workplace.

> But anyone who serves the Lord (wherever they are and whatever they are doing) is in full-time ministry.

As His disciple, what does God want you to do in the workplace? That question is answered through the first thing Christ ever taught His disciples in evangelism. In Matthew 4:19 we are told, "Then He said to them, 'Follow Me, and I will make you fishers of men.'" He wants you to evangelize. When Satan uses the fact that you are not in vocational ministry to intimidate you from engaging in evangelism, he is up to his best at lying and deceiving.

The other thing inherent in this intimidation that Satan uses is to make you think that you must have a volume of knowledge and training to evangelize. The next time Satan causes that thought to come to your mind, ask him a question he will absolutely hate, "Then why is it that new believers, some of whom are not even a week old in the Lord, lead people to Jesus Christ?" It is because they know the only three things you need to know to lead anyone to Jesus Christ: (1) we are sinners; (2) Jesus Christ died for our sins and rose again; and (3) through personal trust in Him alone as our only way to heaven we can receive His free gift of eternal life. New converts share that simple message with family, friends, and co-workers and lead many to Jesus Christ.

To lead someone to Christ, you don't have to know a lot, but you do have to care a lot. No Bible college training or seminary training is required.

Some people do have a specific gift in the area of evangelism. It is seen in their ability to relate to the lost and equip believers in evangelism. Ephesians 4:11–12 tells us, "And He Himself gave some to be apostles, some prophets, some evangelists, and some pastors and teachers, for the equipping of the saints for the work of the ministry, for the edifying of the body of Christ." But nowhere does the Bible say that you have to have that gift in order to evangelize. Sharing your faith is something God has called every believer to do, not just those gifted in evangelism.

In intimidating you with the thought that you need some kind of Bible college or seminary training to evangelize, there is something else Satan never mentions. Sometimes those who are not in vocational Christian work have the best opportunities in evangelism. They are around people every day who need to hear the good news of Christ. People in vocational ministry are often isolated from the people they want to reach. They spend most of their time with believers and lose out on contacts and conversations with unbelievers. You have the advantage every day of being around people who need to hear the gospel.

> Sometimes those who are not in vocational Christian work have the best opportunities in evangelism.

The thought that evangelism is something only gifted evangelists can do or those who have some kind of Bible college or seminary training is one of the most unbiblical thoughts Satan could ever use. It is also proven not to be true by asking and answering the simple question: who leads the most people to Christ? Once more, it is not those who know a lot but those who care a lot. The issue is not, "How much do you know?" but "How much do you care?"

Questions for Reflection

1. Have you looked at yourself each day as someone who is in full-time ministry?

2. Why as a disciple of Christ do you have a responsibility in evangelism even though you may not have the gift of evangelism?

Intimidation #10

Why are you trying to do something that you were a dismal failure at the first time?

God and Satan have one huge thing that shows the difference between them. Satan loves to focus on our past whereas God focuses on our future.

This is a prime example. As you contemplate sharing your faith, Satan loves to remind you of what a "failure" you were the first time. It may be for any number of reasons. Perhaps you were so excited at what you found in Christ that you were a bit blunt or brash in telling family members and friends how much they needed Him. Maybe you mentioned hell in what sounded to them like an uncaring spirit. When they resisted your message and called you a "religious fanatic," you may have even taken offense and had a few choice names to call them. You may have been harsh when you spoke of their lack of interest in the Bible and became angry when they called it a "storybook" with no credibility. As you reflected on what you said or did, you may now view yourself as a failure in evangelism.

That is when Satan loves to come in with his reminders and question you as to why you desire a repeat performance.

Of course, there are several things Satan does not want you to see. One is that, regardless of what you said or did, you were sincere in wanting others to come to faith in Christ. For the first time, you came to realize that you were headed to an eternity without God, and you saw that all change within seconds as you trusted Christ. You were transformed from a kingdom that knew no light to a kingdom that knows no darkness. Colossians 1:13 explains, "He has delivered us from the power of darkness and conveyed us into the kingdom of the Son of His love." Knowing they were headed to that same eternity if they did not trust the Savior, you sincerely wanted something better for them. Your zeal and love overtook your common sense in needing to approach them more tactfully. But what you did was done with sincerity—something that Satan will try his best to keep you from recognizing.

Furthermore, you learned as we all do. Mistakes are one way God teaches us. You are not approaching people the same way today. But remember, Satan capitalizes on the past, not today or tomorrow.

One thing, though, is much larger than all I have mentioned. It is a word Satan would rather you not hear, let alone understand. It is called forgiveness. Colossians 1:14 explains, "In whom we have redemption through His blood, the forgiveness of sins." Forgiveness covers sins—past, present, and future. And once He forgives, He does not dwell on those wrongs anymore. Through the blood shed on the cross, God promises those who come to Him, ". . . For I will forgive their iniquity, and their sin I will remember no more" (Jeremiah 31:34).

> Mistakes are one way God teaches us.

If those sins, failures, mistakes, whatever you would like to call them, are not on His mind, they no longer need to be on yours. As you contemplate sharing your faith, suppose the "failure" you had the first time comes to your mind. Concentrate on the fact that whereas Satan is saying, "Remember?" God is saying, "You are forgiven."

Satan likes to get as much use of the "failure" intimidation as he can. So, he attempts to fill your mind with as many unpleasant thoughts as he can. What if they are forever turned off to any spiritual discussion? What if they never get over the way your abruptness offended them? What if they tell family members what you did, and they get offended as well? In essence, he tries to hold you responsible for their eternal destiny.

The way to confront Satan is with God's truth. Nowhere in the Bible does God hold you or anyone else responsible for someone's eternal destiny. You can only bring Christ to them. You cannot bring them to Christ. Jesus plainly said, "No one can come to Me unless the Father who sent Me draws him; and I will raise him up at the last day" (John 6:44). God is the One who is sovereign, not us. So even if you did a poor job, where that person spends eternity is not on your shoulders.

> Nowhere in the Bible does God hold you or anyone else responsible for someone's eternal destiny.

The bottom line is that you are *never* a failure at sharing your faith. That is simply an intimidation device Satan uses. You ought to be commended for wanting to see anyone come to Christ. You learned through the experience and the tactfulness of your witness has improved. Look for your next opportunity. Keep developing your skills in evangelism. And be grateful that your job is the sharing. God's job is the saving.

Questions for Reflection

1. As you reflect on the past, how has God taught you through your mistakes in evangelism?

2. Why is it wrong to call yourself a failure because of mistakes you made when sharing your faith?

Intimidation #11

People are not approachable; you will be wasting your time.

Satan is jealous of God on many fronts. One of those is omniscience. Although Satan is smart and crafty, He does not know everything. He just likes to pretend he does.

There are two things Satan does in attempting to make use of this intimidation. One is to cause you to think that the people you see in the media are the norm. They may be the *loudest* at times, but they are not the norm. The norm is the person driving to work every morning wondering if the pain he has started to have may be cancer. It is the person who is wondering if the layoff at work that is coming up will include him and is not sure he will have enough to retire on. He drives past a car accident that appears to have a fatality and wonders where he would be if something happened to him. His marriage has been rocky and counseling sessions have done little to help. That fear, anxiety, and insecurity are what God is using to make him receptive to your conversation.

Furthermore, remember that you are making a direct attack on Satan's kingdom when you contemplate sharing your faith. So, another thing he will do is make sure that the first person you approach is the most hardened, closed to the gospel person you will ever meet. He wants to convince you, "That is what they are all like. Lots of luck." He is hoping that first person will be all it takes to cause you to give up.

Confront Satan's lies by talking to those who share Christ on a consistent basis. They will tell you from firsthand experience how few people they meet that are not interested in talking about spiritual things. They will also tell you of those they meet who were appreciative or receptive even if they were not ready at that moment to trust Christ. That is what keeps them moving forward when they do meet someone who has no interest of any kind. They know firsthand that the disinterested person is the exception, not the norm.

> Confront Satan's lies by talking to those who share Christ on a consistent basis.

What Satan will never tell you (and hopes that no one else does either) is that when you are God's servant doing God's thing—reaching out to the lost—you never go it alone. The verses commonly referred to as the Great Commission tell us, "And Jesus came and spoke to them, saying, 'All authority has been given to Me in heaven and on earth. Go therefore and make disciples of all the nations, baptizing them in the name of the Father and of the Son and of the Holy Spirit, teaching them to observe all things that I have commanded you; and lo, I am with you always, even to the end of the age.'" (Matthew 28:18–20)

> God knows that if He will do the preparing, His child will do the talking.

When you are walking in obedience to that assignment, God has all kinds of ways of preparing the people with whom He wants you to share the good news. That is one reason those who are consistent in evangelism have so many good opportunities. God knows that if He will do the preparing, His child will do the talking. Even when they do encounter some resistance, the God who is in them helps them know how to respond as thoughts and ideas come to their minds that they would have never thought of themselves. They experience firsthand the truth of "Lo, I am with you always." So many times, as I have taught evangelism, I have explained situations I was in myself that I had no idea how to respond. But the

God who was in me and with me did. He caused me to think of ideas that I have even shared with others to help them in their own evangelism.

Lastly, remember that Satan is a liar and the father of lies (John 8:44). To tell you that you would be wasting your time with *anyone* is one of his biggest lies. Never in evangelism are you wasting your time with anyone. With every person you share your faith, you learn and you keep on learning. God uses every person you talk to and every experience you have to further equip you.

You are also earning eternal reward because the issue with God is faithfulness, not fruitfulness. 1 Corinthians 4:2 reminds us, "Moreover it is required in stewards that one be found faithful." In every conversation, God is responsible for the results, not you.

> You are also earning eternal reward because the issue with God is faithfulness, not fruitfulness.

Do not let Satan intimidate you with thoughts of who you are likely to find—those who do not want to hear from you. There may be those but that will not be the usual experience. Regardless of who you speak to and their interest or lack of it, you are not wasting your time. You are doing something that God uses to grow you in evangelism and from an eternal perspective that merits great reward and something you will wish you had done more, not less.

Questions for Reflection

1. What might consistency in evangelism prove to you and how will it help you?

2. Why is it never a waste of your time to evangelize?

Intimidation #12

You do not need to use words; your actions are enough.

Anyone who would label Satan as ignorant or stupid doesn't know him. He is a most clever individual. So clever he can say something that sounds good even though it is greatly flawed.

One way he is clever is to say something that sounds like a compliment and then use that as an "excuse" for not evangelizing. That is probably one of the most subtle ways to keep you from evangelizing that he could conceive.

Your life and your actions are important as you share your faith. I question whether any two verses sum it up better than Philippians 2:14–15, "Do all things without complaining and disputing, that you may become blameless and harmless, children of God without fault in the midst of a crooked and perverse generation, among you shine as lights in the world."

Your life gives credibility to what you share. To tell me "Jesus Christ can make a difference in your life" is one thing. To show me how He has made a difference in yours is another.

I am often reminded of the man who came to Christ who attributed his conversion to a neighbor who was very timid. The neighbor expressed surprise saying, "But I never spoke to you about Christ the way I should have." The new convert responded, "No you didn't. But you lived me to death. I could refute others' arguments, and I could upset their logic. But I could not refute the way you lived." In traveling worldwide, I could give you story after story about those who have been drawn to the Savior because they found Jesus Christ so attractive in a believer's life.

To further commend you for the life you live, Satan reminds you of those you met who have said, "I live a better life than most Christians do." He then reminds you that *nobody* can say that of you. So, in essence, he is saying, "You have lived the life you should. You have done enough."

But stop and think about that for a moment. You may have tremendous credibility with unbelievers because you have lived the life a Christian should live. But suppose someone watches you for four minutes, four hours, or four days. They may be impressed with everything you do and even the spirit in which it is done. Would staring at your life explain to them how to get to heaven? Of course not. Even if they stared at a Christian whose life is perfect (which no Christian's is) for an entire year, they wouldn't know how to come to Christ. Someone has to speak to them.

It is interesting that Philippians 2 continues by saying in verse 16, "holding fast the word of life, so that I may rejoice in the day of Christ that I have not run in vain or labored in vain." The word of life refers to the good news of the gospel. The "walking" without the "talking" is of no help to an unbeliever. As we live the life we should, we still need to explain the gospel, that Christ died for us and rose again so that we can enjoy eternity with Him. It is only through hearing that message, receiving it as truth, and responding in faith that they appropriate the gift of eternal life. Hence, Romans 10:17 tells us, "So then faith comes by hearing, and hearing by the word of God."

> Would staring at your life explain to them how to get to heaven?

So, when Satan says, "You do not need to use words, your actions are enough" that is such a subtle tactic. In a clever way, he is trying to get you to live it but not speak it. He knows full well that while living the life might impress them, the one thing he does not want you to do is invite them. Impressing them can be done with the life, but inviting them has to be done with the lips.

> Impressing them can be done with the life, but inviting them has to be done with the lips.

The non-Christian has seen you. You are the one from whom he now has to hear.

Questions for Reflection

1. How does living the life around non-Christians give you even more credibility and opportunity in evangelism?

2. How would you respond to a Christian who believes their moral lifestyle is enough to bring Christ to the lost?

Conclusion

Give God what Satan hates!

One thing Satan hates most in a believer's life is when he or she is obedient to Christ.

The first thing Christ ever taught His disciples was evangelism. He said to them in Matthew 4:19, "Follow Me, and I will make you fishers of men."

Why does Satan hate it when believers follow and fish? There are numerous reasons.

He knows full well that God directs an obedient servant. When we follow Him in evangelism, we learn as we go. What we learn reveals the many things that Satan wants to tell us that are not true. Remember, Satan is a liar and the father of lies. He just wants to intimidate us so that we will freeze up instead of speaking up.

Satan also knows that if we ask Him for it, God will give us boldness in evangelism. All we have to pray is what the disciples prayed, "Now, Lord, look on their threats, and grant to Your servants that with all boldness they may speak Your word" (Acts 4:29). With that boldness, we will be able to put Satan's intimidations behind us and go forth in evangelism.

The Holy Spirit taught the disciples what to say in fearful and difficult situations (Luke 12:12). And Satan knows that God will give you ideas, thoughts, and words that you would have never thought of on your own. The Holy Spirit is the Helper God promises (John 16:7).

So, what is the bottom line? Exactly what God tells us. ". . . He who is in you is greater than he who is in the world" (1 John 4:4). With that in mind, you can move forward in obedience with respect to evangelism thrilled at the prospect of how God is going to use you. With each experience, you can put whatever intimidation Satan wants to use behind you.

Christ in you is greater than he who is in the world and any intimidation Satan attempts to use. Give God your obedience in evangelism and watch how greatly He uses you.

Books by the Author

A Mentor's Wisdom

21 Things God Never Said

31 Days with the Master Fisherman

31 Days to Contagious Living

31 Days Walking with God in the Workplace

31 Days to Living as a New Believer

Show Me How to Share the Gospel

Show Me How to Answer Tough Questions

Show Me How to Share Christ in the Workplace

Show Me How to Preach Evangelistic Sermons

Show Me How to Illustrate Evangelistic Sermons

Free and Clear

101 Tips for Evangelism

The Three Minute Window

Eternal Life: Can you really be certain you have it.

The Unlikely Evangelist

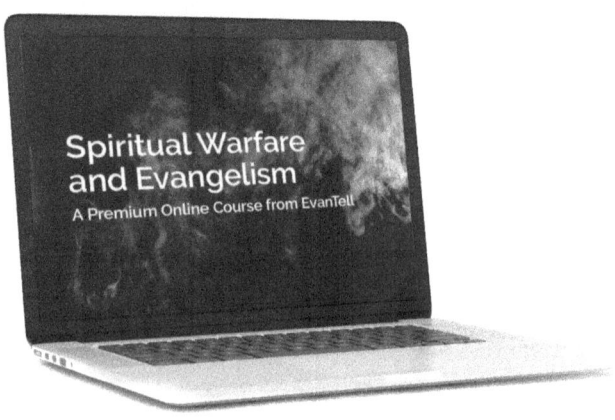

Spiritual Warfare &
Evangelism

A Premium Online Course from EvanTell

Spiritual warfare is a daily reality for everyone who has committed their lives to following Jesus. After completing this course, you will be equipped to recognize spiritual warfare in evangelism, expose the subtle attacks of our enemy, and make full use of the armor of God as you stand firm in your faith.

Take the Interactive Evangelism Training Course at:

EvanTell.org/SpiritualWarfare

THE
EVANGELISM
STUDY BIBLE

Evangelism can mean many things to many people. For some, it's something that requires special training or a calling from God. For others, it's something only done in a church building or arena. And for some, it evokes emotions of guilt and shame for failing to be a vibrant witness to unbelievers.

Using the highly regarded New King James Version, *The Evangelism Study Bible* brings together a wide variety of resources, some never before paired with the text of Scripture.

The Evangelism Study Bible not only provides the training to explain and make clear the good news of the gospel, it also will motivate you to evangelize out of *grace* rather than *guilt*.

Order your copy of *The Evangelism Study Bible* at:

EvanTell.org/store

DOWNLOAD OUR APP
FOR EVANGELISM TRAINING
ON-THE-GO

VISIT YOUR APP STORE
AND SEARCH *"EVANTELL"* TO
DOWNLOAD TODAY

VISIT OUR STORE
FOR BOOKS, TRACTS,
AND MORE RESOURCES

VISIT *EVANTELL.ORG/STORE* TO SEE OUR FULL
COLLECTION OF BOOKS AND RESOURCES

www.ingramcontent.com/pod-product-compliance
Lightning Source LLC
Chambersburg PA
CBHW051550120626
46551CB00013B/1451